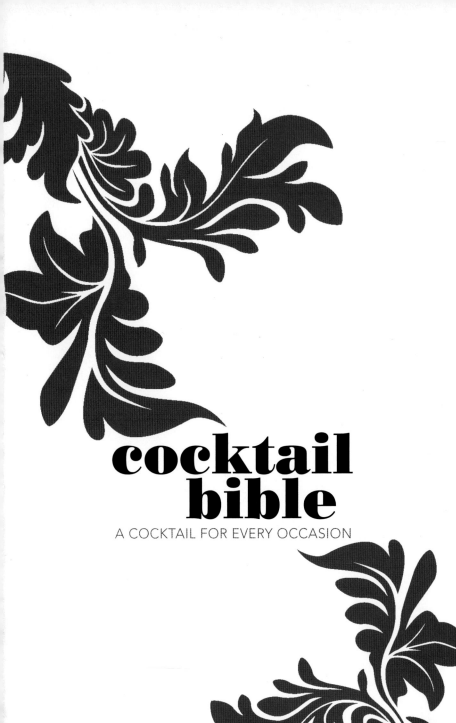

cocktail
bible

A COCKTAIL FOR EVERY OCCASION

cocktail
bible

A COCKTAIL FOR EVERY OCCASION

Bath New York Singapore Hong Kong Cologne Delhi Melbourne

This edition published by Parragon in 2008

Parragon
Queen Street House
4 Queen Street
Bath BA1 1HE, UK

Copyright © Parragon Books Ltd 2007

Design by Talking Design
Photography by Mike Cooper

ISBN: 978-1-4075-3399-5

Printed in China

NOTES FOR THE READER
This book uses metric and imperial measurements. Follow the same units of measurement throughout; do not mix metric and imperial. All spoon measurements are level: teaspoons are assumed to be 5 ml and tablespoons are assumed to be 15 ml. Unless otherwise stated, milk is assumed to be full-fat and eggs are medium-size. Recipes using raw or very lightly cooked eggs should be avoided by infants, the elderly, pregnant and breastfeeding women, convalescents and anyone suffering from an illness. Please consume alcohol responsibly.

CONTENTS

Introduction	06–09
The Classics	10–29
The New Wave	30–47
The Perfect Pick-Me-Up	48–65
Renaissance	66–85
Innovative	86–103
In Vogue	104–121
Party Starter	122–139
Layered Lift-Off	140–157
The Perfect Shot	158–173
Index	174–176

Introduction

Cocktails drift in and out of fashion but their appeal is always to the young or, at least, the young at heart. Making mixed drinks – even the wonderfully colourful and exotic concoctions of the contemporary cocktail bar – isn't difficult and is great fun. Reading the following basic guidelines should ensure you have all the skills of a professional bartender at your fingertips.

Bar Essentials

Cocktail shaker The standard type is a cylindrical metal container with a capacity of 500 ml/18 fl oz that has a double lid incorporating a perforated strainer. To use,

remove the lid, add ice and pour in the ingredients listed in the recipe. Close securely and shake vigorously for 10–20 seconds, until the outside of the shaker is frosted with a fine mist. Remove the small lid and pour the cocktail into the appropriate glass. If your cocktail shaker doesn't have an integral strainer, you will need a separate one. The Boston shaker consists of double conical containers and is designed to be used with a Hawthorn strainer. It's best not to mix more than 2 servings of a cocktail at a time.

Mixing glass This is used for making clear cocktails. It need be no more complicated than the container of your cocktail shaker or a jug about the same size, but you can also buy a professional mixing glass. To use, add ice, pour in the ingredients listed in the recipe and stir vigorously for 20 seconds. Strain into the appropriate glass.

Strainer A bar strainer or Hawthorn strainer is the perfect tool to prevent ice and other unwanted ingredients from being poured from the shaker or mixing

glass into the serving glass. You could also use a small nylon sieve.

Jigger Also called a measure, this small measuring cup is often double-ended and shaped like an hourglass. Standard metric jiggers are 25 ml and 35 ml, while imperial jiggers are 1 fl oz and 1½ fl oz, representing 1 and 1½ measures respectively. The proportions of the various ingredients, but not the specific quantities, are critical, so if you don't have a jigger, you can use the small lid of your cocktail shaker, or a liqueur, schnapps or shot glass, or even a small egg cup.

Bar spoon This long-handled spoon is used for stirring cocktails in a mixing glass.

Muddler This is simply a miniature masher used for crushing ingredients, such as herbs and sugar, in the base of a glass. You can also use a mortar and pestle or even the back of a spoon.

Other basics Lots of ordinary kitchen equipment is useful: 1 or more corkscrews, cocktail sticks,

citrus juicer or reamer, chopping board, some paring, kitchen and canelle knives, a citrus zester, a selection of jugs and a blender for creamy cocktails and slushes. You will also require an ice bucket and tongs – never pick up ice with your fingers. Optional extras include swizzle sticks and straws.

Glasses

Champagne flute Tall thin stemmed glass holding 125–150 ml/ 4–5 fl oz.

Cocktail glass Stemmed glass with a cone-shaped bowl holding 125–150 ml/4–5 fl oz.

Collins glass Tall, narrow glass with straight sides, usually holding 300 ml/10 fl oz.

Goblet Short-stemmed glass with a large bowl holding 300 ml/10 fl oz.

Highball glass Tall, straight glass holding 225 ml/8 fl oz.

Margarita glass Stemmed glass with a small bowl topped with a wide saucer shape.

Old-fashioned glass Chunky glass holding 225 ml/8 fl oz.

Shot glass Small glass holding 50 ml/2 fl oz, suitable for shooters.

Bartender's Tips

Sugar syrup Even fine caster sugar often fails to dissolve completely in the brief time that a cocktail is shaken or stirred, so it is better to use sugar syrup or syrop de gomme when sweetening drinks. To make this, put 4 tablespoons caster sugar and 4 tablespoons water into a small saucepan. Gradually bring to the boil over a low heat, stirring constantly until the sugar has dissolved. Boil, without stirring, for 1–2 minutes, then and leave to cool. Store in a sterilized jar or bottle in the refrigerator for up to 2 months.

Chilling For absolute perfection you should chill spirits, mixers and serving glasses in the refrigerator. However, it's not always possible to find room for glasses and you should never put fine crystal in the refrigerator. As an alternative, fill glasses with cracked ice, stir well, then tip out the ice and any water before pouring in the cocktail.

Frosting glasses You can use caster sugar, fine salt or desiccated coconut to decorate the rim of a glass. Rub the rim with a little lemon or lime juice and then dip the glass upside down into a shallow saucer containing your chosen decoration.

Layering (pousse-café) To make a multi-layered drink, slowly pour the liqueurs or spirits, in the order specified in the recipe, over the back of a teaspoon into the glass. Each layer then settles on top of the layer before it.

Ice To crack ice, put cubes in a strong plastic bag and hit with the smooth side of a meat mallet or a rolling pin. Alternatively, bang the bag against a wall. Ice can be crushed in a food processor or blender. To store large quantities of ice, place the cubes in a strong plastic bag and before returning them to the freezer squirt with soda water to stop the cubes from sticking together.

The Classics

Martini

FOR MANY, THIS IS THE ULTIMATE COCKTAIL. IT IS NAMED AFTER ITS
INVENTOR, MARTINI DE ANNA DE TOGGIA, NOT THE FAMOUS BRAND
OF VERMOUTH!

SERVES 1
3 measures gin
1 tsp dry vermouth, or to taste
cracked ice cubes
green cocktail olive, to
 decorate

1 Shake the gin and
 vermouth over cracked
 ice until well frosted.
2 Strain into a chilled
 cocktail glass and dress
 with the cocktail olive.

Daiquiri

DAIQUIRI IS A TOWN IN CUBA, WHERE THIS DRINK WAS SAID TO HAVE
BEEN INVENTED IN THE EARLY PART OF THE TWENTIETH CENTURY. A
BUSINESSMAN HAD RUN OUT OF IMPORTED GIN AND SO HAD TO MAKE
DO WITH THE LOCAL DRINK – RUM – WHICH, AT THAT TIME, WAS OFTEN
OF UNRELIABLE QUALITY.

SERVES 1
2 measures white rum
¾ measure lime juice
½ tsp sugar syrup
cracked ice

1 Pour the rum, lime
   juice and sugar syrup
   over ice and shake
   vigorously until well
   frosted.
2 Strain into a chilled
   cocktail glass.

Manhattan

SAID TO HAVE BEEN INVENTED BY SIR WINSTON CHURCHILL'S AMERICAN MOTHER, JENNIE, THE MANHATTAN IS ONE OF MANY COCKTAILS NAMED AFTER PLACES IN NEW YORK.

SERVES 1
dash Angostura bitters
3 measures rye whisky
1 measure sweet vermouth
cracked ice cubes
cocktail cherry, to decorate

1 Shake the liquids over cracked ice in a mixing glass and mix well.
2 Strain into a chilled glass and decorate with the cherry.

Sangria

A PERFECT LONG COLD DRINK FOR A CROWD OF FRIENDS AT A
SUMMER BARBECUE!

SERVES 6
juice of 1 orange
juice of 1 lemon
2 tbsp caster sugar
ice cubes
1 orange, thinly sliced
1 lemon, thinly sliced
1 bottle red wine, chilled
lemonade

1 Shake the orange and
  lemon juice with the
  sugar and transfer to a
  large bowl or jug.
2 When the sugar has
  dissolved, add a few
  ice cubes, sliced fruit
  and wine.
3 Marinate for 1 hour if
  possible, and then add
  lemonade to taste and
  more ice.

Mimosa

SO CALLED BECAUSE IT RESEMBLES THE COLOUR OF A MIMOSA'S
ATTRACTIVE YELLOW BLOOM.

SERVES 1
flesh of 1 passion fruit
½ measure orange Curaçao
crushed ice
champagne, chilled
slice of star fruit, to decorate

1 Scoop out the passion fruit flesh into a jug or shaker and shake with the Curaçao and a little crushed ice until frosted.
2 Pour into the base of a champagne flute and top up with champagne.
3 Decorate with the slice of star fruit.

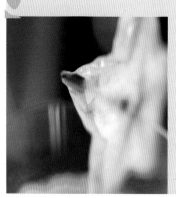

Bellini

THIS DELICIOUS CONCOCTION WAS CREATED BY GIUSEPPE CIPRIANI AT HARRY'S BAR IN VENICE, AROUND 1943.

SERVES 1

1 measure fresh peach juice made from lightly sweetened liquidized peaches
caster sugar
3 measures champagne, chilled

1 Dip the rim of a champagne flute into some peach juice and then into the sugar to create a sugar-frosted effect. Set aside to dry. Chill.
2 Pour the peach juice into the chilled flute and stir gently.
3 Top up with champagne.

Margarita

THIS COCKTAIL, ATTRIBUTED TO FRANCISCO MORALES AND INVENTED IN 1942 IN MEXICO, IS A MORE CIVILIZED VERSION OF THE ORIGINAL WAY TO DRINK TEQUILA – A LICK OF SALT FROM THE BACK OF YOUR HAND, A SUCK OF LIME JUICE AND A SHOT OF TEQUILA!

SERVES 1
lime wedge
coarse salt
3 measures white tequila
1 measure Triple Sec or
    Cointreau
2 measures lime juice
cracked ice cubes
slice of lime, to decorate

1 Rub the rim of a chilled cocktail glass with the lime wedge and then dip in a saucer of coarse salt to frost.
2 Shake the tequila, Triple Sec and lime juice vigorously over cracked ice until well frosted.
3 Strain into the prepared glass and decorate with the slice of lime.

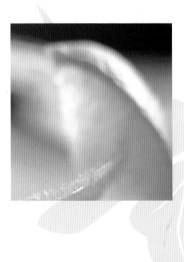

Club Mojito

DARK RUM IS RICH IN FLAVOUR AND REDOLENT OF SUNSHINE HOLIDAY MEMORIES.

SERVES 1
1 tsp syrop de gomme
few mint leaves, plus extra
   to decorate
juice ½ lime
ice
2 measures Jamaican rum
soda water
dash Angostura bitters

1 Put the syrop, mint leaves and lime juice into a glass and muddle the mint leaves.
2 Add the ice and rum and shake well, pour into a cocktail glass and top up with soda water to taste.
3 Finish with a dash of Angostura bitters and decorate with the remaining mint leaves.

Mai Tai

CREATED IN 1944 BY RESTAURATEUR 'TRADER VIC' IT WAS DESCRIBED AS 'MAI TAI – ROE AE' MEANING 'OUT OF THIS WORLD'. IT IS ALWAYS FLAMBOYANTLY DRESSED.

SERVES 1
2 measures white rum
2 measures dark rum
1 measure orange Curaçao
1 measure lime juice
1 tbsp orgeat
1 tbsp grenadine
cracked ice cubes
slices of pineapple, pieces
  of fruit peel, cocktail
  cherries and straws, to
  decorate

1 Shake the white and dark rums, Curaçao, lime juice, orgeat and grenadine vigorously over ice until well frosted.
2 Strain into a chilled glass and decorate as you wish.

The New Wave

Mudslide

DESPITE ITS OMINOUS-SOUNDING NAME, THIS IS A RICHLY FLAVOURED
CREAMY CONCOCTION THAT IS DELICIOUS WHATEVER THE WEATHER.

SERVES 1
1½ measures Kahlúa
1½ measures Baileys Irish
   Cream
1½ measures vodka
cracked ice cubes

1 Shake the Kahlúa,
  Baileys Irish Cream and
  vodka vigorously over
  ice until well frosted.
2 Strain into a chilled
  glass.

Mint Julep

A JULEP IS SIMPLY A MIXED DRINK SWEETENED WITH SYRUP. THE MINT JULEP WAS PROBABLY FIRST MADE IN THE UNITED STATES, AND IS THE TRADITIONAL DRINK OF THE KENTUCKY DERBY.

SERVES 1
leaves from 1 fresh mint sprig,
plus extra to decorate
1 tbsp sugar syrup
crushed ice cubes
3 measures bourbon whiskey

1 Put the mint leaves and sugar syrup into a small chilled glass and mash with a teaspoon.
2 Add the crushed ice and shake to mix, before adding the bourbon.
3 Decorate with the remaining mint leaves.

White Lady

SIMPLE, ELEGANT, SUBTLE AND MUCH MORE POWERFUL THAN APPEARANCE SUGGESTS, THIS IS THE PERFECT COCKTAIL TO SERVE BEFORE AN AL FRESCO SUMMER DINNER.

SERVES 1
2 measures gin
1 measure Triple Sec
1 measure lemon juice
cracked ice cubes

1 Shake the gin, Triple Sec and lemon juice vigorously over ice until well frosted.
2 Strain into a chilled cocktail glass.

Kamikaze

NO TURNING BACK ON THIS ONE. IT'S SO DELICIOUS – YOU WON'T BE
ABLE TO PUT IT DOWN!

SERVES 1
1 measure vodka
1 measure Triple Sec
½ measure fresh lime juice
½ measure fresh lemon juice
ice
dry white wine, chilled
pieces of lime and
   cucumber, to decorate

1 Shake the first four
   ingredients together
   over ice until well
   frosted.
2 Strain into a chilled
   glass and top up with
   wine.
3 Dress with the lime and
   cucumber.

Black Widow

NOT AS WICKED AS ITS TITLE SUGGESTS, BUT IF YOU ARE FEELING
ADVENTUROUS YOU COULD TAKE IT STRAIGHT, ON THE ROCKS!

SERVES 1
⅔ measure dark rum
⅓ measure Southern
   Comfort
juice ½ lime
dash Curaçao
ice
soda water
lime peel, to decorate

1 Shake the first four
   ingredients together
   well over ice and strain
   into a chilled tumbler.
2 Top up with soda water
   to taste and decorate
   with the lime peel.

Indian Summer

THE COFFEE LIQUEUR IS THE KEY INGREDIENT IN THIS DELICIOUS LONG MIX – IT WOULD BE GOOD WITH CRÈME DE NOYEAU OR CRÈME DE CACAO, TOO.

SERVES 1
1 measure vodka
2 measures Kahlúa
1 measure gin
2 measures pineapple juice
ice
tonic water

1 Shake the first four ingredients well over ice until frosted.
2 Strain into a medium cocktail glass or wine glass and top up with tonic water to taste.

Ocean Breeze

IT'S A BREEZE TO MAKE AND AS COLOURFUL AS THE WHIPPED-UP
OCEAN ON AN EARLY MORNING. JUST DON'T DILUTE IT TOO MUCH.

SERVES 1
1 measure white rum
1 measure amaretto
½ measure blue Curaçao
½ measure pineapple juice
crushed ice
soda water

1 Shake the first four
   ingredients together
   over ice.
2 Pour into a tall glass
   and top up with soda
   water to taste.

Whiskey Sour

ORIGINATING IN THE AMERICAN SOUTH AND USING SOME OF THE BEST AMERICAN WHISKEY, THIS CLASSIC CAN ALSO BE MADE WITH VODKA, GIN OR OTHER SPIRITS.

SERVES 1
1 measure lemon or lime
    juice
2 measures blended whiskey
1 tsp caster sugar or syrop
    de gomme
ice
slice of lime or lemon, to
    decorate
maraschino cherry, to
    decorate

1 Shake the first three
    ingredients well over
    ice and strain into a
    cocktail glass.
2 Decorate with the slice
    of lime or lemon, and
    the cherry.

The Perfect Pick-Me-Up

White Cosmopolitan

NOTHING LIKE ITS PINK COUSIN THE COSMOPOLITAN, FOR THIS IS FAR
MORE FRUITY AND, INSTEAD OF VODKA, IT IS BASED ON A PUNCHY
LEMON-FLAVOURED LIQUEUR.

SERVES 1
1½ measures limoncello
½ measure Cointreau
1 measure white cranberry
  and grape juice
ice
dash orange bitters
few red cranberries, to
  decorate

1 Shake the first three
  ingredients over ice
  until frosted.
2 Strain into a chilled
  cocktail glass.
3 Add a dash of bitters
  and dress with the
  cranberries.

Pink Squirrel

CRÈME DE NOYEAU HAS A WONDERFUL, SLIGHTLY BITTER, NUTTY
FLAVOUR BUT IS, IN FACT, MADE FROM PEACH AND APRICOT KERNELS.
IT IS USUALLY SERVED AS A LIQUEUR, BUT DOES COMBINE WELL WITH
SOME OTHER INGREDIENTS IN COCKTAILS.

SERVES 1
2 measures dark crème de
  cacao
1 measure crème de noyeau
1 measure single cream
cracked ice cubes

1 Shake the crème
  de cacao, crème de
  noyeau and single
  cream vigorously over
  ice until well frosted.
2 Strain into a chilled
  cocktail glass.

Deauville Passion

DEAUVILLE WAS ELEGANT, EXTRAVAGANT AND VERY FASHIONABLE
DURING THE COCKTAIL ERA EARLY LAST CENTURY AND NO DOUBT
MANY GREAT COCKTAILS WERE CREATED THERE.

SERVES 1
1¾ measures cognac
1¼ measures apricot
  Curaçao
1¼ measures passion-fruit
  juice
ice
bitter lemon, to taste
mint leaves, to decorate

1 Shake the first three
ingredients over ice
until well frosted.
2 Strain into a chilled
glass and top up with
the bitter lemon, to
taste.
3 Decorate with the mint
leaves.

Zombie

THE INDIVIDUAL INGREDIENTS OF THIS COCKTAIL, INCLUDING LIQUEURS AND FRUIT JUICES, VARY CONSIDERABLY FROM ONE RECIPE TO ANOTHER, BUT ALL ZOMBIES CONTAIN A MIXTURE OF WHITE, GOLDEN AND DARK RUM IN A RANGE OF PROPORTIONS.

SERVES 1
2 measures dark rum
2 measures white rum
1 measure golden rum
1 measure Triple Sec
1 measure lime juice
1 measure orange juice
1 measure pineapple juice
1 measure guava juice
1 tbsp grenadine
1 tbsp orgeat
1 tsp Pernod
crushed ice cubes
sprigs of fresh mint and
  pineapple wedges, to
  decorate

1 Shake all the liquids together over crushed ice until smooth.
2 Pour, without straining, into a chilled glass.
3 Decorate with the mint and the pineapple wedges.

Adam 'n' Eve

DON'T EXPECT THIS COCKTAIL TO BE FULL OF APPLES! THE BASE IS SHARP AND ASTRINGENT, WHILST THE TOP IS SWEET AND FROTHY – NO DISCRIMINATION HERE, OF COURSE!

SERVES 1
2 measures Triple Sec
1 measure vodka
1 measure grapefruit juice
1 measure cranberry juice
ice
5-6 cubes pineapple
2 tsp caster sugar
crushed ice
slice of strawberry, to decorate

1 Shake the first four ingredients over ice until well frosted.
2 Strain into a chilled glass.
3 In a blender, whizz the pineapple with sugar and 1–2 tbsp of crushed ice to a frothy slush.
4 Float gently on the top of the cocktail.
5 Dress with a slice of strawberry.

Orange Blossom

DURING THE PROHIBITION YEARS IN THE USA, GIN WAS OFTEN QUITE
LITERALLY MADE IN THE BATHTUB AND FLAVOURED WITH FRESH
ORANGE JUICE TO CONCEAL ITS FILTHY FLAVOUR. MADE WITH GOOD-
QUALITY GIN, WHICH NEEDS NO SUCH CONCEALMENT, THIS DRINK IS
DELIGHTFULLY REFRESHING.

SERVES 1
2 measures gin
2 measures orange juice
cracked ice cubes
slice of orange, to decorate

1 Shake the gin and
orange juice vigorously
over ice until well
frosted.

2 Strain into a chilled
cocktail glass and
decorate with the
orange slice.

Moonlight

THIS LIGHT WINE-BASED COCKTAIL IS AN IDEAL DRINK TO MAKE FOR SEVERAL PEOPLE.

SERVES 4
3 measures grapefruit juice
4 measures gin
1 measure kirsch
4 measures white wine
½ tsp lemon zest
ice

1 Shake the first five ingredients well over ice and strain into chilled glasses.

Cherry Kitch

THIS IS A VELVETY SMOOTH COCKTAIL, FRUITY BUT WITH A RICH BRANDY
UNDERTONE. A TOUCH OF MARASCHINO LIQUEUR ADDED AT THE END
WOULD BE GOOD, TOO.

SERVES 1
1 measure cherry brandy
2 measures pineapple juice
½ measure kirsch
1 egg white
1 scoop crushed ice
frozen maraschino cherry, to
    decorate

1 Shake the first four
   ingredients well over
   ice until frosted.
2 Pour into a chilled tall
   thin glass and decorate
   with the frozen
   maraschino cherry.

Renaissance

Cosmopolitan

INVITING AND REFRESHING, THE COSMOPOLITAN IS THE BEVERAGE
OF CHOICE FOR THE 'SEX AND THE CITY' GIRLS AND IS A MUST AT ANY
FASHIONABLE PARTY.

SERVES 1
2 measures vodka
1 measure Triple Sec
1 measure fresh lime juice
1 measure cranberry juice
ice
strip of orange peel

1 Shake all the liquid
  ingredients over ice
  until well frosted.
2 Strain into a chilled
  cocktail glass.
3 Dress with the strip of
  orange peel.

Sex On The Beach

HOLIDAY DRINKS ARE OFTEN LONG AND FRUITY AND THIS REFRESHING
COCKTAIL IS REMINISCENT OF HAPPY DAYS IN THE SUN.

SERVES 1
1 measure peach schnapps
1 measure vodka
2 measures fresh orange juice
3 measures cranberry and
    peach juice
ice and crushed ice
dash of lemon juice
piece of orange peel, to
    decorate

1 Shake the first four
    ingredients over ice
    until well frosted.
2 Strain into a glass
    filled with crushed iced
    and squeeze over the
    lemon juice.
3 Dress with the orange
    peel.

Harvey Wallbanger

THIS WELL-KNOWN CONTEMPORARY CLASSIC COCKTAIL IS A GREAT PARTY DRINK – MIX IT STRONG AT FIRST, THEN WEAKER AS THE EVENING GOES BY – OR WITHOUT ALCOHOL FOR DRIVERS AND NO ONE WOULD KNOW!

SERVES 1
ice cubes
3 measures vodka
8 measures orange juice
2 tsp Galliano
cherry and slice of orange,
  to decorate

1 Half fill a glass with ice, pour vodka and orange over the ice cubes, and float Galliano on top.

2 Garnish with the cherry and the slice of orange.

3 For a warming variant, mix a splash of ginger wine with the vodka and orange.

Bloody Mary

THIS CLASSIC COCKTAIL WAS INVENTED IN 1921 AT THE LEGENDARY
HARRY'S BAR IN PARIS. THERE ARE NUMEROUS VERSIONS – SOME MUCH
HOTTER AND SPICIER THAN OTHERS. INGREDIENTS MAY INCLUDE
HORSERADISH SAUCE IN ADDITION TO OR INSTEAD OF TABASCO SAUCE.

SERVES 1
dash Tabasco sauce
dash Worcestershire sauce
cracked ice cubes
2 measures vodka
splash dry sherry
6 measures tomato juice
juice ½ lemon
pinch celery salt
pinch cayenne pepper
celery stick with leaves, to
　decorate
slice of lemon, to decorate

1 Dash the
　Worcestershire sauce
　and Tabasco sauce
　over ice in a shaker and
　add the vodka, splash
　of dry sherry, tomato
　juice and lemon juice.
2 Shake vigorously until
　frosted.
3 Strain into a tall chilled
　glass, add a pinch
　of celery salt and a
　pinch of cayenne and
　decorate with the
　celery stick and the
　slice of lemon.

Slow Comfortable Screw

ALWAYS USE FRESHLY SQUEEZED ORANGE JUICE TO MAKE THIS
REFRESHING COCKTAIL – IT IS JUST NOT THE SAME WITH BOTTLED
JUICE. THIS SIMPLE, CLASSIC COCKTAIL HAS GIVEN RISE TO NUMEROUS
AND INCREASINGLY ELABORATE VARIATIONS.

SERVES 1
2 measures sloe gin
orange juice
cracked ice cubes
slice of orange, to decorate

1 Shake the sloe gin
and orange juice over
ice until well frosted
and pour into a chilled
glass.
2 Decorate with the slice
of orange.

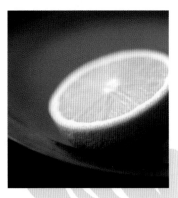

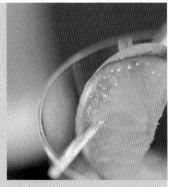

Long Island Iced Tea

DATING BACK TO THE DAYS OF THE AMERICAN PROHIBITION, WHEN IT WAS DRUNK OUT OF CUPS IN AN ATTEMPT TO FOOL THE FBI THAT IT WAS HARMLESS, THIS COCKTAIL HAS EVOLVED FROM THE ORIGINAL SIMPLE COMBINATION OF VODKA WITH A DASH OF COLA!

SERVES 1
2 measures vodka
1 measure gin
1 measure white tequila
1 measure white rum
½ measure white crème de
   menthe
2 measures lemon juice
1 tsp sugar syrup
cracked ice cubes
cola
slice of lime or lemon, to
   decorate

1 Shake the vodka, gin, tequila, rum, crème de menthe, lemon juice and sugar syrup vigorously over ice until well frosted.

2 Strain into an ice-filled glass and top up with cola.

3 Dress with the lime or lemon slice.

Screwdriver

THIS COCKTAIL HAS UNIVERSAL APPEAL, AND IS GREAT TO SERVE TO
GUESTS AT A PARTY IF YOU ARE NOT SURE OF INDIVIDUAL TASTES.
FRESHLY SQUEEZED ORANGE JUICE IS A MUST.

SERVES 1
cracked ice cubes
2 measures vodka
orange juice
slice of orange, to decorate

1 Fill a chilled glass with
   cracked ice cubes.
2 Pour the vodka over
   the ice and top up with
   orange juice.
3 Stir well to mix and
   dress with the slice of
   orange.

Seabreeze

PINK GRAPEFRUIT JUICE IS MUCH SWEETER AND SUBTLER THAN ITS
PALER COUSIN, SO IT IS IDEAL TO MIX IN COCKTAILS WHERE YOU WANT
JUST A SLIGHT SHARPNESS.

SERVES 1
1½ measures vodka
½ measure cranberry juice
ice
pink grapefruit juice, to taste

1 Shake the vodka and
  cranberry juice over ice
  until frosted.
2 Pour into a chilled
  tumbler or long glass
  and top up with pink
  grapefruit juice to
  taste.

Black Russian

HISTORY RECORDS ONLY WHITE AND RED RUSSIANS. THE OMISSION OF THE BLACK RUSSIAN IS A SAD OVERSIGHT. FOR A COFFEE LIQUEUR, YOU CAN USE EITHER TIA MARIA OR KAHLÚA, DEPENDING ON YOUR PERSONAL TASTE – THE LATTER IS SWEETER.

SERVES 1
2 measures vodka
1 measure coffee liqueur
4-6 cracked ice cubes

1 Pour the vodka and liqueur over cracked ice cubes in a small chilled glass.

2 Stir to mix.

Innovative

Blue Monday

THE LOVELY COLOUR AND FRUITY FLAVOUR OF THIS COCKTAIL IS
GUARANTEED TO MAKE MONDAY YOUR FAVOURITE DAY OF THE WEEK.

SERVES 1
cracked ice
1 measure vodka
½ measure Cointreau
1 tbsp blue Curaçao

1 Put the cracked ice
 into a mixing glass or
 jug and pour in the
 vodka, Cointreau and
 Curaçao.
2 Stir well and strain into
 a cocktail glass.

Fuzzy Navel

THIS IS ANOTHER COCKTAIL WITH A NAME THAT PLAYS ON THE
INGREDIENTS – FUZZY TO REMIND YOU THAT IT CONTAINS PEACH
SCHNAPPS AND NAVEL BECAUSE IT IS MIXED WITH ORANGE JUICE.

SERVES 1
2 measures vodka
1 measure peach schnapps
250ml/9 fl oz orange juice
cracked ice cubes
physalis (cape gooseberry),
   to decorate

1 Shake the vodka,
   peach schnapps and
   orange juice vigorously
   over cracked ice until
   well frosted.
2 Strain into a chilled
   cocktail glass and
   decorate with the
   physalis.

Golden Frog

AS A RULE, CLASSIC VODKA COCKTAILS WERE INTENDED TO PROVIDE AN ALCOHOLIC DRINK WITH NO TELL-TALE SIGNS ON THE BREATH AND WERE USUALLY FAIRLY SIMPLE MIXES OF NON-ALCOHOLIC FLAVOURS. CONTEMPORARY VODKA COCKTAILS OFTEN INCLUDE OTHER SPIRITS.

SERVES 1
ice cubes
1 measure vodka
1 measure Strega
1 measure Galliano
1 measure lemon juice

1 Whizz 4–6 ice cubes in a blender with the vodka, Strega, Galliano and lemon juice.
2 Blend until slushy.
3 Pour into a chilled cocktail glass.

Moscow Mule

THIS COCKTAIL CAME INTO EXISTENCE THROUGH A HAPPY
COINCIDENCE DURING THE 1930S. AN AMERICAN BAR OWNER HAD
OVERSTOCKED GINGER BEER AND A REPRESENTATIVE OF A SOFT
DRINKS COMPANY INVENTED THE MOSCOW MULE TO HELP HIM OUT.

SERVES 1
2 measures vodka
1 measure lime juice
cracked ice cubes
ginger beer
slice of lime, to decorate

1 Shake the vodka and
  lime juice vigorously
  over ice until well
  frosted.
2 Half-fill a chilled
  cocktail glass with
  cracked ice cubes and
  strain the cocktail over
  them.
3 Top up with ginger
  beer. Dress with the
  slice of lime.

Peartini

WHILE LESS POPULAR THAN PEACH OR CHERRY EAU DE VIE, PEAR BRANDY HAS A DELICATE FRAGRANCE AND LOVELY FLAVOUR, BUT DON'T CONFUSE IT WITH PEAR LIQUEUR.

SERVES 1
1 tsp caster sugar
pinch of ground cinnamon
1 lemon wedge
cracked ice
1 measure vodka
1 measure pear brandy, such as Poire William or Pera Segnana

1 Mix together the sugar and cinnamon on a saucer. Rub the outside rim of a cocktail glass with the lemon wedge, then dip it into the sugar and cinnamon mixture. Set aside.
2 Put the cracked ice into a mixing glass or jug and pour in the vodka and pear brandy. Stir well and strain into the prepared glass, without disturbing the frosting.

Salty Dog

WHEN THIS COCKTAIL FIRST APPEARED, GIN-BASED MIXES WERE BY FAR THE MOST POPULAR, BUT NOWADAYS A SALTY DOG IS MORE FREQUENTLY MADE WITH VODKA. CHOOSE WHICHEVER YOU PREFER, BUT THE COCKTAILS WILL HAVE DIFFERENT FLAVOURS.

SERVES 1
1 tbsp granulated sugar
1 tbsp coarse salt
lemon half
6-8 cracked ice cubes
2 measures vodka
grapefruit juice

1 Mix the sugar and salt in a saucer. Rub the rim of a chilled cocktail glass with the lemon half, then dip it in the sugar and salt mixture to frost.
2 Fill the glass with cracked ice cubes and pour the vodka over them.
3 Top up with grapefruit juice and stir to mix. Drink with a straw.

Spotted Bikini

A CHEEKY NAME FOR AN AMUSING COCKTAIL. IT ALSO TASTES GREAT, ALTHOUGH YOU MAY LIKE TO ADD A LITTLE SUGAR TO TASTE.

SERVES 1
2 measures vodka
1 measure white rum
1 measure cold milk
juice ½ lemon
ice
1 ripe passion fruit
piece of lemon, to decorate

1 Shake the first four ingredients over ice until well frosted.
2 Strain into a chilled medium cocktail glass and add the passion fruit, not strained, at the last minute so you see the black seeds.
3 Dress with the piece of lemon.

Woo-woo

BE SURE TO WOO YOUR FRIENDS WITH THIS REFRESHING AND SIMPLE
DRINK. IT'S ALSO GREAT FOR PARTIES.

SERVES 1
cracked ice cubes
2 measures vodka
2 measures peach schnapps
4 measures cranberry juice
physalis (cape gooseberry), to
   decorate

1 Half-fill a chilled
  cocktail glass with
  cracked ice.
2 Pour the vodka, peach
  and cranberry juice
  over the ice.
3 Stir well to mix and
  decorate with the
  physalis.

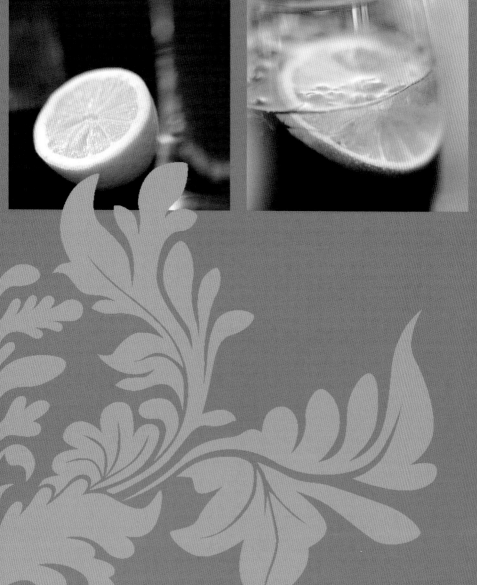

In Vogue

Vodkatini

A CERTAIN MR BOND POPULARISED THE USE OF VODKA AS THE BASE OF THE MARTINI, RATHER THAN GIN, HENCE THE VODKATINI IS NOW WIDELY ACCEPTED AS AN INCREDIBLY STYLISH AND TASTY ALTERNATIVE.

SERVES 1
1 measure vodka
ice
dash dry vermouth
a twist of lemon peel or a
    single olive, to decorate

1 Pour the vodka over a handful of ice in a mixing glass.
2 Add the vermouth, stir well and strain into a cocktail glass.
3 Dress with the lemon peel.

Vodka Espresso

THIS WOULD MAKE A FABULOUS AFTER-DINNER TREAT. IT'S USUALLY MADE WITH STOLICHNAYA VODKA AND AMARULA, A SOUTH AFRICAN CREAM LIQUEUR WITH A CARAMEL FLAVOUR.

SERVES 1
cracked ice
2 measures espresso or other
   strong brewed coffee,
   cooled
1 measure vodka
2 tsp caster sugar
1 measure Amarula

1 Put the cracked ice into a cocktail shaker, pour in the coffee and vodka and add the sugar.
2 Cover and shake vigorously for 10–20 seconds, until the outside of the shaker is misted.
3 Strain into a cocktail glass, then float the Amarula on top.

Flying Grasshopper

THERE ARE TWO VERSIONS OF THIS COCKTAIL – ONE MADE WITH EQUAL
QUANTITIES OF WHITE AND GREEN CRÈME DE MENTHE, AND ONE WITH
GREEN CRÈME DE MENTHE AND CHOCOLATE LIQUEUR.

SERVES 1
cracked ice
1 measure vodka
1 measure green crème de
menthe
1 measure white crème de
menthe

1 Put the cracked ice
into a mixing glass or
pitcher and pour in the
vodka and crème de
menthe. Stir well and
strain into a glass.

Flirtini

THIS COMBINATION OF VODKA AND CHAMPAGNE IS GUARANTEED TO
BRINK A SPARKLE TO THE EYES AND A SMILE TO THE LIPS – WHAT COULD
BE MORE ATTRACTIVE?

SERVES 1
¼ slice fresh pineapple,
  chopped
½ measure chilled Cointreau
½ measure chilled vodka
1 measure chilled pineapple
  juice
chilled champagne or sparkling
  white wine, to top up

1 Put the pineapple
  and Cointreau into a
  mixing glass or jug and
  muddle with a spoon
  to crush the pineapple.
2 Add the vodka and
  pineapple juice and stir
  well, then strain into a
  champagne flute.
3 Top up with
  champagne.

Bullshot

THIS IS NOT UNLIKE DRINKING CHILLED CONSOMMÉ – BUT WITH A NOTICEABLE KICK. IT IS BEST REALLY COLD.

SERVES 1
1 measure vodka
2 measures beef consommé
    or good stock
dash fresh lemon juice
2 dashes Worcestershire
    sauce
ice
celery salt
strip of lemon peel, to
    decorate

1 Shake all the liquid ingredients well with ice and strain into a glass with extra ice.
2 Sprinkle with celery salt and dress with the strip of lemon peel.

Cranberry Collins

THE CLASSIC COLLINS DRINK IS MADE WITH GIN, BUT ITS MANY
VARIATIONS ARE MADE WITH OTHER SPIRITS SO TRY THIS ONE FOR SIZE...

SERVES 1
2 measures vodka
¾ measure elderflower
   cordial
3 measures white cranberry
   and apple juice or to taste
ice
soda water
slice of lime, to decorate

1 Shake the first three
   ingredients over ice
   until well frosted.
2 Strain into a glass with
   more ice and top up
   with soda to taste.
3 Dress with the slice
   of lime.

Silver Berry

THIS DRINK IS PERFECT FOR ONE OF THOSE VERY SPECIAL OCCASIONS –
EXCEPT THAT YOU REALLY CAN'T DRINK VERY MANY!

SERVES 1
1 measure raspberry vodka,
  iced
1 measure crème de cassis,
  iced
1 measure Cointreau, iced
frozen berry, to decorate

1 Carefully and slowly
  layer the three liquors
  in the order listed, in a
  well-iced shot glass or
  tall thin cocktail glass.
2 They must be well iced
  first and may need
  time to settle into their
  layers.
3 Dress with the frozen
  berry.

Metropolitan

THIS SOPHISTICATED COCKTAIL FOR CITY SLICKERS SHARES ITS NAME, BUT NOT ITS INGREDIENTS, WITH AN EQUALLY URBANE CLASSIC FROM THE PAST.

SERVES 1
1 lemon wedge
1 tbsp caster sugar
cracked ice
½ measure vodka or lemon vodka
½ measure crème de framboise or other raspberry liqueur
½ measure cranberry juice
½ measure orange juice
2 cranberries, to decorate

1 Rub the outside rim of a glass with the lemon wedge and dip it into the sugar to frost. Set aside.
2 Put the cracked ice into a cocktail shaker and pour in the vodka, liqueur, cranberry juice and orange juice.
3 Cover and shake vigorously for 10–20 seconds, until the outside of the shaker is misted.
4 Strain into the prepared glass, taking care not to disturb the frosting, and decorate with the cranberries.

Party Starter

Tequila Slammer

SLAMMERS ARE ALSO KNOWN AS SHOOTERS. THE IDEA IS THAT YOU
POUR THE INGREDIENTS DIRECTLY INTO THE GLASS, WITHOUT STIRRING.
COVER THE GLASS WITH ONE HAND TO PREVENT SPILLAGE, SLAM IT
ON TO A TABLE TO MIX AND DRINK THE COCKTAIL DOWN IN ONE! DO
ENSURE YOU USE A STRONG GLASS!

SERVES 1
1 measure white tequila, chilled
1 measure lemon juice
sparkling wine, chilled

1 Put the tequila and
  lemon juice into a
  chilled glass.
2 Top up with sparkling
  wine.
3 Cover the glass with
  your hand and slam.

Brain Haemorrhage

THIS IS A RARE INSTANCE OF A COCKTAIL THAT IS DELIBERATELY INTENDED TO LOOK HORRID, RATHER THAN TEMPTING, AND WAS PROBABLY INVENTED TO DRINK AT HALLOWEEN.

SERVES 1
1 measure chilled peach schnapps
1 tsp chilled Baileys Irish Cream
½ tsp chilled grenadine

1 Pour the peach schnapps into a shot glass, then carefully float the Baileys on top. Finally, top with the grenadine.

Toffee Split

YOU SHOULD NOT NEED A DESSERT AS WELL, BUT YOU COULD ALWAYS POUR THIS OVER SOME ICE CREAM.

SERVES 1
crushed ice
2 measures Drambuie
1 measure toffee liqueur,
  iced

1 Fill a small cocktail glass or shot glass with crushed ice.
2 Pour on the Drambuie and pour in the toffee liqueur carefully from the side of the glass so it layers on top.
3 Drink immediately.

B-52

THE B-52 WAS CREATED IN THE FAMOUS ALICE'S RESTAURANT IN MALIBU, CALIFORNIA. THE NAME REFERS TO THE US B-52 STRATOFORTRESS LONG-RANGE BOMBER.

SERVES 1

1 measure chilled dark crème de cacao

1 measure chilled Baileys Irish Cream

1 measure chilled Grand Marnier

1 Pour the crème de cacao into a shot glass.

2 With a steady hand, gently pour in the Baileys Irish Cream to make a second layer, then gently pour in the Grand Marnier.

3 Cover and slam.

Alabama Slammer

SMALL, BUT PERFECTLY PROPORTIONED – THIS IS A SHOOTER WITH A REAL KICK!

SERVES 1
1 measure Southern Comfort
1 measure amaretto
½ measure sloe gin
½ tsp lemon juice

1 Pour the Southern Comfort, amaretto and sloe gin over cracked ice in a mixing glass and stir.
2 Strain into a shot glass and add ½ tsp lemon juice.
3 Cover and slam.

White Diamond Frappé

THIS IS A CRAZY COMBINATION OF LIQUEURS, BUT IT WORKS WELL
ONCE YOU'VE ADDED THE LEMON. EXTRA CRUSHED ICE AT THE LAST
MINUTE BRINGS OUT ALL THE SEPARATE FLAVOURS.

SERVES 1
¼ measure peppermint
schnapps
¼ measure white crème de
cacao
¼ measure anise liqueur
¼ measure lemon juice
ice and crushed ice

1 Shake all the liquid
ingredients over ice
until frosted.
2 Strain into a chilled
glass and add a small
spoonful of crushed
ice.

Cowboy

IN MOVIES, COWBOYS DRINK THEIR RYE STRAIGHT, OFTEN PULLING
THE CORK OUT OF THE BOTTLE WITH THEIR TEETH. IT IS CERTAINLY
DIFFICULT TO IMAGINE JOHN WAYNE OR CLINT EASTWOOD SIPPING
DELICATELY FROM A CHILLED COCKTAIL GLASS.

SERVES 1
3 measures rye whiskey
2 tbsp single cream
cracked ice cubes

1 Pour the whiskey and
cream over ice and
shake vigorously until
well frosted.
2 Strain into a chilled
glass.

After Five

ORIGINALLY THE NAME OF A MIXED COCKTAIL TOPPED UP WITH LEMONADE OR SODA, IT HAS NOW BEEN COMPLETELY TRANSFORMED INTO A LAYERED SHOOTER WITH A REAL KICK.

SERVES 1
½ measure chilled
   peppermint schnapps
1 measure chilled Kahlúa
1 tbsp chilled Baileys Irish
   Cream

1 Pour the peppermint schnapps into a shot glass. Carefully pour the Kahlúa over the back of a teaspoon so that it forms a separate layer.
2 Finally, float the Baileys Irish Cream on top.

Layered Lift-Off

Pousse-Café

A POUSSE-CAFÉ IS A LAYERED COCKTAIL OF MANY DIFFERENT
COLOURED LIQUEURS. IT IS CRUCIAL TO ICE ALL THE LIQUEURS FIRST.

SERVES 1
¼ measure grenadine
¼ measure crème de menthe
¼ measure Galliano
¼ measure kümmel
¼ measure brandy

1 Ice all the liqueurs and
a tall shot, cocktail or
pousse-café glass.
2 Carefully pour the
liqueurs over a spoon
evenly into the glass.
3 Leave for a few
minutes to settle.

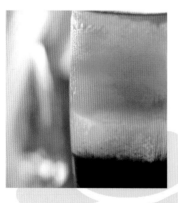

Aurora Borealis

THIS SPECTACULAR, COLOURED DRINK SHOULD NOT BE MIXED OR STIRRED. LEAVE IT TO SWIRL AROUND THE GLASS, CREATING A MULTI-HUED EFFECT AND TRY TO GUESS THE VARIOUS FLAVOURS.

SERVES 1
1 measure iced grappa or
  vodka
1 measure iced green
  Chartreuse
½ measure iced orange
  Curaçao
few drops iced cassis

1 Pour the grappa slowly round one side of a well-chilled shot glass.
2 Gently pour the Chartreuse round the other side.
3 Pour the Curaçao gently into the middle and add a few drops of cassis just before serving. Don't stir. Drink slowly!

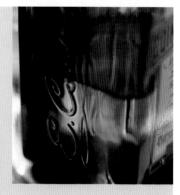

Nuclear Fallout

THIS IS SIMILAR TO A POUSSE-CAFÉ, WHERE THE LIQUEURS ARE
LAYERED, BUT, IN THIS CASE, THE HEAVIEST LIQUEUR IS COLDEST AND
ADDED LAST, TO CREATE THE SLOW DROPPING EFFECT.

SERVES 1
1 tsp raspberry syrup
¼ measure maraschino
¼ measure yellow
   Chartreuse
¼ measure Cointreau
½ measure well-iced blue
   Curaçao

1 Chill all the liqueurs but
   put the blue Curaçao
   in the coldest part of
   the freezer. Also chill
   a shot, pousse-café or
   elgin glass.
2 Carefully pour the
   drinks in layers over
   the back of a teaspoon
   except the blue
   Curaçao.
3 Finally, pour in the blue
   Curaçao and wait for
   the fallout!

Stars and Swirls

YOU WILL NEED A STEADY HAND FOR THIS ONE – PREFERABLY TWO
PAIRS OF STEADY HANDS.

SERVES 1
1 measure Malibu
large ice cube
½ measure strawberry or
   raspberry liqueur
1 tsp blue Curaçao

1 Chill a small shot glass
   really well.
2 Pour in the Malibu and
   add a large ice cube.
3 Carefully pour in the
   other two liqueurs from
   opposite sides of the
   glass very slowly so
   they fall down the sides
   and swirl around.

Fancy Free

THE KEY TO THIS LAYERED DRINK IS TO ICE THE LIQUEUR AND ICE THE GLASS. IF IT DOES SEEM TO MIX ON IMPACT, GIVE IT A LITTLE TIME TO SETTLE AND FORM ITS LAYERS AGAIN.

SERVES 1
⅓ measure cherry brandy, iced
⅓ measure Cointreau, iced
⅓ measure apricot liqueur, iced

1 Pour the three liqueurs in order into an iced elgin, tall shot glass or liqueur glass. Carefully pour them over the back of a spoon so they form coloured layers.

Fifth Avenue

AFTER-DINNER COCKTAILS OFTEN INCLUDE CREAM AND THIS ONE ALSO
HAS THE DELICATE FLAVOURS OF APRICOT AND COCOA.

SERVES 1
1 measure dark crème de
  cacao, iced
1 measure apricot brandy,
  iced
1 measure cream

1 Pour the ingredients,
  one at a time, into a
  chilled tall cocktail
  glass. Pour the layers
  slowly over the back of
  a spoon resting against
  the edge of the glass.
  Each layer should float
  on top of the previous
  one.

African Mint

AMARULA IS A VERY RICH AND EXOTIC LIQUEUR, WHICH IS BEST SERVED AND DRUNK REALLY COLD – BUT NOT ON ICE BECAUSE THAT WILL DILUTE ITS REAL CHARACTER.

SERVES 1
¾ measure crème de menthe, chilled
¾ measure Amarula, chilled

1 Pour the crème de menthe into the base of a shot glass or slim cocktail glass, saving a few drops.
2 Pour the Amarula slowly over the back of a spoon to create a layer over the mint.
3 Drizzle any remaining drops of mint over the creamy liqueur to finish.

Napoleon's Nightcap

INSTEAD OF HOT CHOCOLATE, NAPOLEON FAVOURED A CHOCOLATE-LACED BRANDY WITH A HINT OF BANANA. DARING AND EXTRAVAGANT!

SERVES 1
1¼ measures cognac
1 measure dark crème de
  cacao
¼ measure crème de banane
ice
1 tbsp cream

1 Stir the first three
  ingredients in a mixing
  glass with ice.
2 Strain into a chilled
  cocktail glass and
  spoon on a layer of
  cream.

Perfect Love

THIS IS THE LITERAL TRANSLATION FOR AN UNUSUAL PURPLE LIQUEUR
FLAVOURED WITH ROSE PETALS, ALMONDS AND VANILLA.

SERVES 1
1 measure vodka
½ measure Parfait Amour
½ measure maraschino
scoop of crushed ice

1 Shake all the liquid
   ingredients together
   over ice until frosted.
2 Strain into a chilled tall
   thin cocktail glass with
   more ice.

Jealousy

THIS REALLY IS AN AFTER-DINNER COCKTAIL AND IF YOU WANT A
CHANGE, YOU COULD OCCASIONALLY FLAVOUR THE CREAM WITH A
DIFFERENT LIQUEUR.

SERVES 1
1 tsp crème de menthe
1–2 tbsp double cream
2 measures coffee or
    chocolate liqueur
crushed ice
chocolate matchsticks, to
    serve

1 Gently beat the mint
    liqueur into the cream
    until thick.
2 Pour the coffee liqueur
    into a very small iced
    glass and carefully
    spoon on the whipped
    flavoured cream.
3 Serve with chocolate
    matchsticks.

Tequila Shot

ACCORDING TO CUSTOM THIS IS THE ONLY WAY TO DRINK NEAT TEQUILA. IT IS OFTEN DESCRIBED AS BEING SMOOTH AND TART, SO ADDING LIME JUICE AND SALT MAY SOUND CONTRADICTORY, BUT IT WORKS!

SERVES 1
1 measure gold tequila
pinch salt
wedge of lime

1 Pour tequila into a shot glass.
2 Put the salt at the base of your thumb, between thumb and forefinger.
3 Hold the lime wedge in the same hand.
4 Hold the shot in the other hand.
5 Lick the salt, down the tequila and suck the lime.

Voodoo

THIS ENTHRALLING MIXTURE OF FLAVOURS IS GUARANTEED TO WEAVE
A SPELL ON YOUR TASTE BUDS AND WORK ITS MAGIC FROM THE VERY
FIRST SIP.

SERVES 1
½ measure chilled Kahlúa
½ measure chilled Malibu
½ measure chilled
   butterscotch schnapps
1 measure chilled milk

1 Pour the Kahlúa,
Malibu, schnapps and
milk into a glass and
stir well.

Margarita Jelly Shot

IT IS NOT ESSENTIAL TO FROST THE GLASSES WITH SALT BUT IT DOES
LOOK ATTRACTIVE AND PAYS HOMAGE TO THE ORIGINAL NON-JELLY
COCKTAIL RECIPE OF 1942.

SERVES 10
½ lime, cut into wedges
2 tbsp fine salt
1 packet lime jelly
300 ml/10 fl oz hot water
4–5 tbsp Cointreau
200–250 ml/7–9 fl oz tequila

1 Rub the outside rims
of 10 glasses with the
lime wedges, then
dip in the salt to frost
them. Set aside.
2 Break up the jelly and
place it in a heatproof
measuring jug. Pour
in the hot water and
stir until the jelly has
dissolved. Leave until
cool, then stir in the
Cointreau and tequila
to make the mixture up
to 600 ml/1 pint.
3 Divide among the
prepared glasses,
taking care not
to disturb the salt
frosting, and chill in the
refrigerator until set.

Peppermint Patty

SOMETIMES THE SIMPLE THINGS IN LIFE ARE THE BEST – ONE SUCH
PLEASURE IS THIS DELICIOUS COMBINATION OF CHOCOLATE AND
PEPPERMINT.

SERVES 1
cracked ice
1 measure white crème de
cacao
1 measure white crème de
menthe

1 Put the ice in a cocktail
shaker and pour in the
crème de cacao and
crème de menthe.
2 Close the shaker and
shake vigorously for
10–20 seconds, until
the outside of the
shaker is misted.
3 Strain into a shot glass
or cocktail glass.

Zipper

THIS SHOOTER GETS ITS NAME FROM AN UNUSUAL, NOT TO SAY
"LOUCHE" METHOD OF SERVING IT, BUT TASTES JUST AS GOOD SERVED
MORE CONVENTIONALLY.

SERVES 1
crushed ice
1 measure tequila
½ measure Grand Marnier
½ measure single cream

1 Put the crushed ice
into a cocktail shaker
and pour in the tequila,
Grand Marnier and
cream. Close the
shaker and shake
vigorously for 10–20
seconds, until the
outside of the shaker
is misted. Strain into a
shot glass.

Index

A
Adam 'n' Eve 58
African Mint 154
After Five 138
Alabama Slammer 132
amaretto
    Alabama Slammer 132
    Ocean Breeze 44
Amarula
    African Mint 154
    Vodka Espresso 108
anise: White Diamond Frappé 134
Aurora Borealis 144

B
B-52 130
Baileys Irish Cream
    After Five 138
    B-52 130
    Brain Haemorrhage 126
    Mudslide 32
Bellini 22
Black Russian 84
Black Widow 40
Bloody Mary 74
Blue Monday 88
Brain Haemorrhage 126
brandy
    Cherry Kitch 64
    Deauville Passion 54
    Fancy Free 150
    Fifth Avenue 152
    Napoleon's Nightcap 156
    Peartini 96
    Pousse-Café 142
Bullshot 114

C
champagne
    Bellini 22
    Flirtini 112
    Mimosa 20
Chartreuse
    Aurora Borealis 144
    Nuclear Fallout 146
Cherry Kitch 64
chocolate liqueur: Jealousy 162
Club Mojito 26
coffee liqueur
    Black Russian 84

Jealousy 162
see also Kahlúa
Cointreau
    Blue Monday 88
    Fancy Free 150
    Flirtini 112
    Margarita 24
    Margarita Jelly Shot 168
    Nuclear Fallout 146
    Silver Berry 118
    White Cosmopolitan 50
Cosmopolitan 68
Cowboy 136
Cranberry Collins 116
crème de banane:
    Napoleon's Nightcap 156
crème de cacao
    B-52 130
    Fifth Avenue 152
    Flying Grasshopper 110
    Napoleon's Nightcap 156
    Peppermint Patty 170
    Pink Squirrel 52
    White Diamond Frappé 134
crème de cassis: Silver Berry 118
crème de framboise: Metropolitan 120
crème de menthe
    African Mint 154
    Flying Grasshopper 110
    Jealousy 162
    Long Island Iced Tea 78
    Peppermint Patty 170
    Pousse-Café 142
crème de noyeau: Pink Squirrel 52
Curaçao
    Aurora Borealis 144
    Black Widow 40
    Blue Monday 88
    Deauville Passion 54
    Mai Tai 28
    Mimosa 20
    Nuclear Fallout 146
    Ocean Breeze 44
    Stars and Swirls 148

D
Daiquiri 14
Deauville Passion 54
Drambuie: Toffee Split 128

F
Fancy Free 150
Fifth Avenue 152
Flirtini 112
Flying Grasshopper 110
Fuzzy Navel 90

G
Galliano
    Golden Frog 92
    Harvey Wallbanger 72
    Pousse-Café 142
gin
    Alabama Slammer 132
    Indian Summer 42
    Long Island Iced Tea 78
    Martini 12
    Moonlight 62
    Orange Blossom 60
    Slow Comfortable Screw 76
    White Lady 36
ginger beer: Moscow Mule 94
Golden Frog 92
Grand Marnier
    B-52 130
    Zipper 172
grappa: Aurora Borealis 144

H
Harvey Wallbanger 72

I
Indian Summer 42

J
Jealousy 162

K
Kahlúa
    After Five 138
    Indian Summer 42
    Mudslide 32
    Voodoo 166
Kamikaze 38
kirsch
    Cherry Kitch 64
    Moonlight 62
kümmel: Pousse-Café 142

L
Limoncello: White Cosmopolitan 50
Long Island Iced Tea 78

M
Mai Tai 28
Malibu
    Stars and Swirls 148
    Voodoo 166
Manhattan 16
maraschino
    Nuclear Fallout 146
    Perfect Love 160
Margarita 24
Margarita Jelly Shot 168
Martini 12
Metropolitan 120
Mimosa 20
Mint Julep 34
Moonlight 62
Moscow Mule 94
Mudslide 32

N
Napoleon's Nightcap 156
Nuclear Fallout 146

O
Ocean Breeze 44
Orange Blossom 60

P
Parfait Amour: Perfect Love 160
Peartini 96
Peppermint Patty 170
Perfect Love 160
Pernod: Zombie 56
Pink Squirrel 52
Pousse-Café 142

R
red wine: Sangria 18
rum
    Black Widow 40
    Club Mojito 26
    Daiquiri 14
    Long Island Iced Tea 78
    Mai Tai 28
    Ocean Breeze 44
    Spotted Bikini 100
    Zombie 56

S
Salty Dog 98
Sangria 18
schnapps
　After Five 138
　Brain Haemorrhage 126
　Fuzzy Navel 90
　Sex On The Beach 70
　Voodoo 166
　White Diamond Frappé 134
　Woo-Woo 102
Screwdriver 80
Seabreeze 82
Sex On The Beach 70
sherry: Bloody Mary 74
Silver Berry 118
Slow Comfortable Screw 76
Southern Comfort
　Alabama Slammer 132
　Black Widow 40
Spotted Bikini 100
Stars and Swirls 148
Strega: Golden Frog 92

T
tequila
　Long Island Iced Tea 78
　Margarita 24
　Margarita Jelly Shot 168
　Tequila Shot 164
　Tequila Slammer 124
　Zipper 172
Toffee Split 128
Triple Sec
　Adam 'n' Eve 58
　Cosmopolitan 68
　Kamikaze 38
　Margarita 24
　White Lady 36
　Zombie 56

V
vermouth
　Manhattan 16
　Martini 12
　Vodkatini 106
vodka
　Adam 'n' Eve 58
　Aurora Borealis 144
　Black Russian 84
　Bloody Mary 74
　Blue Monday 88

Bullshot 114
Cosmopolitan 68
Cranberry Collins 116
Flirtini 112
Flying Grasshopper 110
Fuzzy Navel 90
Golden Frog 92
Harvey Wallbanger 72
Indian Summer 42
Kamikaze 38
Long Island Iced Tea 78
Metropolitan 120
Moscow Mule 94
Mudslide 32
Peartini 96
Perfect Love 160
Salty Dog 98
Screwdriver 80
Seabreeze 82
Sex On The Beach 70
Silver Berry 118
Spotted Bikini 100
Vodkatini 106
Woo-Woo 102
Vodka Espresso 108
Vodkatini 106
Voodoo 166

W
whisky
　Cowboy 136
　Manhattan 16
　Mint Julep 34
　Whiskey Sour 46
White Cosmopolitan 50
White Diamond Frappé 134
White Lady 36
white wine
　Flirtini 112
　Kamikaze 38
　Moonlight 62
　Tequila Slammer 124
Woo-Woo 102

Z
Zipper 172
Zombie 56